Get AHEAD in
COMPUTING

Great
GAMES

Clive Gifford

WAYLAND

First published in 2017 by Wayland

Copyright © Hodder and Stoughton, 2017

Wayland
Carmelite House
50 Victoria Embankment
London EC4Y 0DZ

Wayland Australia
Level 17/207 Kent Street
Sydney, NSW 2000

Produced for Wayland by
White-Thomson Publishing Ltd
www.wtpub.co.uk
01273 479982

Project Editor: Sonya Newland
Designer: Rocket Design (East Anglia) Ltd

A catalogue record for this title is available
from the British Library.

ISBN: 978 1 5263 0402 5

Printed in China

Wayland, part of Hachette Children's Group
and published by Hodder and Stoughton Limited
www.hachette.co.uk

All images courtesy of Shutterstock except:
Alamy: p.13b (Reuters), p.16 (Ian Dagnall), p.18b (Reuters); iStock: p.9br (LICreate),
p.10b (klerik78), p.15b (ilbusca), p.18t (PandaWild), p.27b (Maxiphoto); Wikimedia: p.7t
(Pargon), p.27t (Jordifferer).

Note to readers: Words highlighted in bold appear in the Glossary on page 30.
Answers to activities are on page 31.

Contents

Fun on the Screen

Computer games (also known as video games) are a type of computer program. They are made up of lines of computer code that instruct the computer, arcade machine or games **console**. Games were once only played in black and white on large, silent computers in businesses and colleges. Today, they blaze with colour and action, roar with sound, and are played all over the place!

Big business

Computer gaming is now a major industry. There are more than 2,400 computer-game companies in the UK alone. New games are launched with a splash of publicity, just like major movies. It is big business: global computer-game sales were US$91 billion in 2015.

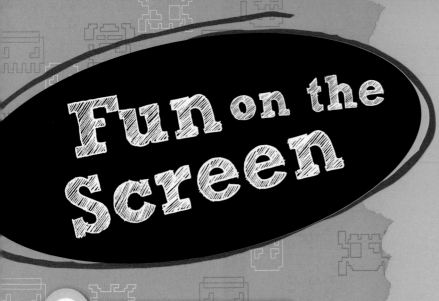

COMPUTER Hero!

Most computer games today are the work of a large team of people, but the first version of Minecraft was created and coded by just one person — **Markus Persson** from Sweden (known as Notch) — in 2009. Persson wrote his first, simple computer game at the age of eight!

Markus Persson

Games everywhere

Games can be played on personal computers, laptops and tablets. They can also be played on smartphones or handheld games consoles when users are on the move. When a game is made, it is often converted so that it can work on lots of different machines. This is called **porting**.

The falling-blocks puzzle game Tetris was invented in 1984.

TRUE STORY

Out of this World! The first game to be played in space was Tetris — a falling-blocks puzzle game invented in 1984. Nine years later, it was played by astronaut Aleksandr Serebrov on a Nintendo Game Boy (a handheld games machine) on the Russian MIR space station.

Meet and Greet

Many gamers (game players) compete against one another in games competitions. Gamers and games makers often meet at events called conventions. The world's biggest gaming convention is Gamescom, which is held in the German city of Cologne each year. In 2016, 345,000 people turned up!

Early Computer Games

Electronic computers were first built and used in the 1940s, during the Second World War. The work of these early machines was deadly serious, such as doing the maths to predict where a cannon shell would fly. But it wasn't long before some programmers started having some fun …

The first games

In 1950, Bertie the Brain was demonstrated in Canada. This 4-metre-high computer could play a human at noughts and crosses. Other early games were draughts and simple chess programs. Usually, only scientists or students got to play them, because at the time computers were rare and expensive. Most were found in the military, government departments or universities.

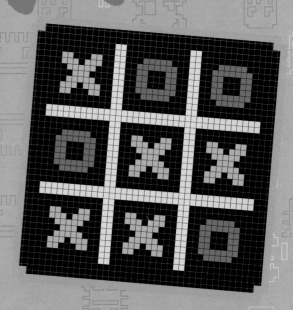

Spacewar!

Coded by American college student Steve Russell and friends, Spacewar! was the first computer action game. This type of game is now known as an arcade game. It was first played in 1962, and featured two battling spaceships on a PDP-1 computer's small, round screen.

Gaming boom

Computer games boomed in the late 1970s and 1980s. More and more people gained access to computers, and handheld games machines became popular. As computers became more powerful, creators were able to make games that were more colourful and detailed.

COMPUTER Hero!

Nolan Bushnell enjoyed playing Spacewar! at college and, with Ted Dabney, he designed a version called Computer Space. It was the first commercially sold coin-operated game to appear in arcades. In 1977, his company, Atari, released the bestselling Atari 2600 console. This plugged into a home TV screen and introduced computer games such as Space Invaders and Pac-Man to millions of people.

The Computer Space arcade game

STRETCH YOURSELF

Make History

Can you match the games invention to the correct date? (You can find the answers on page 31.)

1972, 1981, 1983, 1989, 1994, 2005, 2006, 2009

☞ a) Angry Birds is released and helps create a boom in games played on smartphones and tablets.

☞ b) The first Sony PlayStation is launched. It uses compact discs to store games programs.

☞ c) The first **3D** game, 3D Monster Maze, is released.

☞ d) Pong becomes one of the first coin-operated computer games in arcades.

☞ e) The first Nintendo Wii consoles go on sale.

☞ f) Snipes becomes the first game played by players in different places all connected to the **Internet**.

☞ g) The first Guitar Hero game is released, with a guitar-shaped **game controller**.

☞ h) The Game Boy is released and becomes the world's most popular handheld games machine.

7

Types of Games

There are many types, or genres, of games. Here are some of the most popular genres.

⬇ Traditional and puzzle games

These include card games such as solitaire and snap, puzzle games such as Candy Crush Saga, and board games such as chess and draughts. Many of these games involve the computer acting as an opponent against the player.

⬇ Sports and racing

From FIFA 17 and NBA Live to Wii Sports Resort, many games allow people to play a computer version of a sport. Racing games let gamers race cars, motorbikes, skateboards and many other vehicles on tracks or through scenes.

⬇ Shooters

This popular genre includes classic games such as Defender and adult games such as Call of Duty and Halo. Some show the action from above. Others are first-person shooters (FPS), where the game's scenes are displayed as if looking through the character's eyes.

Platform games

Characters in these games have to jump, duck, run and swing to move between platforms, pass obstacles and overcome enemies to travel through the game's levels. Super Mario 64, Tomb Raider and the Rayman series are popular platform games.

Adventure and sandbox games

In adventure games, players follow a story, meet other characters and solve puzzles to complete a quest or task. Sandbox games, such as Minecraft, also have a world to explore. However, these games are open-ended, which means that there is more than one way to complete the game.

Simulations

Simulation games mimic a real-life situation, such as owning a pet or flying an aircraft. Some, like SimCity, give players the task of building a town or, like Madden NFL, running an American Football team.

Rhythm games

Games like Guitar Hero and Just Dance challenge a player's timing and sense of rhythm. Players have to match on-screen moves to dance or play tunes, sometimes as part of a group.

Storyboards

The action and the sequence of events in a game have to be carefully planned and mapped out. One way to do this is to create **storyboards**, which act as a visual script or plan of the game's action.

Finding your way

Storyboards allow games designers to move scenes or different parts of action around to get the order and story correct before they begin coding. Some games makers use storyboards as a way of judging how the gameplay might work on a particular level or part of their game. For example, on a platform or maze game, they may sketch out all the different routes through a level to help them judge whether they are too easy or difficult.

Silver-screen storyboarding

Storyboarding was first developed by the makers of animated movies (cartoons). Walt Disney and his team used this technique a lot from the 1930s onwards, and then makers of live-action movies began using it too. Directors would use sketches of each scene to work out how to position lighting and cameras. They also used them to show the cast and crew how the film's scenes would look and how the story would progress.

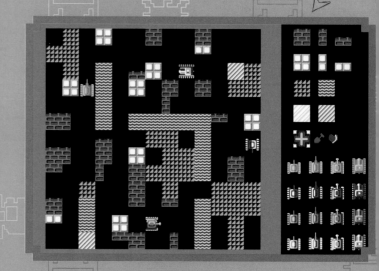

Cutscenes

Many computer games feature **cutscenes**. The action in a cutscene may further the game's story a little, show characters talking to one another, or give the player clues or tips. Lengthy, detailed cutscenes for major games are storyboarded just like the game action. Pac-Man and Space Invaders II were among the first major games to feature cutscenes.

STRETCH YOURSELF

Your Own Storyboard

To get an idea of how storyboarding works, grab some large sheets of paper and draw four, six or eight equal-sized rectangles on each. These are your blank storyboards. Pick a fairy tale, fable or another short story you have read, and try to tell the story in 16 separate storyboard entries or less.

You can use arrows on the scenes to show movement and write short notes underneath each image. Don't worry if you're not the world's best artist, just sketch in each scene to tell the story. Think about the following:

☞ How will you set the scene at the start?

☞ How will the characters or objects move around?

☞ If there are different scenes, how will you move between them?

☞ Will there be jokes or a surprise ending?

☞ What sort of celebration cutscene would you show after a player has completed a game or a level successfully?

Game Assets

All the things viewed in a computer game – characters, vehicles, obstacles, tools and weapons – are known as **assets**. They are first designed by artists. Then they are turned into digital form by modellers and coders so that they can work, move and react in the game.

 ## Early game art

The first computer action games, like Computer Space and Pong, were black and white because the screens they were displayed on could not show colour. Even when colour games arrived in the 1970s, their assets were made up of large blocks. This is because the screens could only show low numbers of **pixels**. As computers have increased in power and screen resolution, the quality of computer-game graphics has improved dramatically.

TRUE STORY

Bad Memory? Games in the past had to be coded to run on small amounts of computer **memory**. The smash hit platform game Super Mario Bros occupied just 31 kilobytes (kb) of memory. A modern game can be a million times that size!

Gamers try out an old-fashioned game on a black-and-white screen.

Games artists

Games artists illustrate the different assets in a game, from scenery to weapons. Important game characters usually get the most attention and can take weeks to get right. But everything that a player interacts with in the game is designed with care.

level 0 90
level 1 135
level 2 285

3D assets

Many modern games are three dimensional, so the game's assets have to be turned into 3D models that can be viewed from any angle. 3D modelling frequently creates a sort of skeleton or outline of the asset. Hinges (also known as hinge points or **avars**) are added to these models, which allow programmers to write code that will alter these points to move parts of the object during the game. The outer surface of the asset is added using texturing programs, which can mimic all sorts of materials.

SOUND, SPEECH AND MUSIC

The sounds and speech that occur in a game are assets as well. Just like graphics, these have to be planned and produced. Modern games have a lot of dialogue. The action role-playing game Fallout 4, for example, contains more than 111,000 spoken lines. These all have to be recorded by voice actors.

Motion capture

One way of creating a 3D computer model is motion capture. Human actors wear a special suit, often fitted with strips or balls, which show up when the actor is filmed making movements. These movements are translated into computer data, which is then turned into animated 3D models for use in the game. Motion capture is often used in sports simulation and fighting games to create realistic-looking movement.

13

Game Characters

Most games feature characters of some kind, and a lot of thought goes into the characters for a major game. Teams of artists make hundreds of sketches before they hit upon the right design.

Big impact

Some characters not only star in their game but also become gaming icons. These include Pac-Man, Red (below) from the Angry Birds game and Mario, the plump plumber with a moustache. He first appeared in the 1981 game Donkey Kong. Gamers loved him and he has since appeared in more than 200 other games, as well as starring in his own movie and TV show!

Cast of characters

In most games, the user plays a particular character. However, there is usually a wide range of other characters too. NPCs (non-player characters) are controlled by the computer. Some NPCs may be allies or friends of the main game character. Others are opponents, which a player's character must avoid or defeat in order to progress in the game.

Bosses

Bosses are characters that are found near the end of a level in many games. They are harder to defeat than other opponents and represent the biggest challenge before a gamer can move on to the next level. One famous boss is Bowser (right), who is found in many Mario and Super Mario games.

STRETCH YOURSELF

Create a Character!

Grab some paper and design three of your own computer game characters: a hero or heroine, who will be the gamer's character, a baddie who gets in the way or chases the hero, and a boss who must be confronted at the end of the game. Ask yourself these questions:

☞ What special abilities might each character have?

☞ How would the character stand out against the game background?

☞ What clothing would they wear?

☞ What accessories or tools would they carry?

☞ How would they use them in the game?

☞ What strengths and weaknesses would each character have?

TRUE STORY

A Slice of History. The famous Pac-Man character was invented by the Japanese games designer Toru Iwatani while he was eating his dinner! He was inspired by the shape of a pizza when a slice is removed.

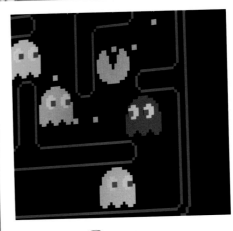

Pac-Man

15

The Game World

Most computer games are set in an imaginary world. This may be as small and simple as the room in which a card game is played, or it could be made up of hundreds of different locations in which many adventures take place.

Setting the scene

The game world includes the setting of the game. For example, a racing game or maze game might be set on a fantasy planet, in a jungle, a haunted house or even under water. The game world creates atmosphere as well as providing the space through which a player's character travels.

Big world

Some games have giant game worlds. World of Warcraft is a **massively multi-player online role-playing game (MMORPG)**. The original game world had 1,400 different locations, which took 150 people more than four years to build. The finished game contained 5.5 million lines of computer code!

SIMULATION GAME WORLDS

In simulation games – those that simulate real-life places – the game world must be realistic and accurate. This can be a huge task in a big game like Microsoft's Flight Simulator X. This has 24,000 different airports for players to fly to, all modelled on real places.

Level up

Many games are divided up into sections known as levels. Players usually have to complete or reach a certain score on one level before moving on to the next. A good game gradually increases the difficulty as the player rises through the levels, providing them with new and tougher challenges.

TRUE STORY

Ruler of Games! King Games created the smash hit puzzle game Candy Crush Saga in 2012. Since then they have continued to add levels for players to enjoy. By the start of 2017, the game boasted 2,845 levels!

On the Level

Design a level of a platform game. Decide on the setting for the game and create the background. Then add the platforms and think of ways the character can move between platforms around the level. Ask yourself these questions:

☞ Is your game world going to be flat or three dimensional (3D)?

☞ What materials will each platform be made of?

☞ How many different routes around the level will there be?

☞ What obstacles and threats will you put in the character's way?

☞ How will you make the level that follows it slightly more difficult?

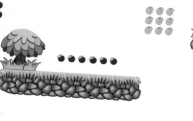

Game Rules and Features

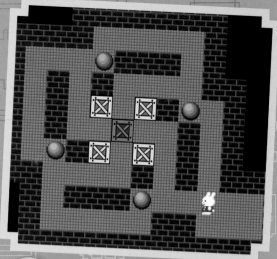

Every computer game has its own rules – the things players can and cannot do within the game. When you think up and design your first game, you have to create these rules. You also need to consider what other features will make your game fun and really playable.

 Fair play

A good game sets players challenges, but also gives them a chance to succeed. After all, if the game is too difficult, players probably won't come back for more! For example, in a maze game there must be a way out that the player can find. If a game includes enemies, there must be a way for the player's character to either avoid or defeat them.

COMPUTER Hero!

Lucy Bradshaw

Thinking up and making computer games is certainly not just for boys! American programmer **Lucy Bradshaw** helped design and create The Sims family simulation game, which was a huge hit. She also helped produce Sim City 3000, Spore, and Dragon Age: Inquisition.

Power-ups

Power-ups are little bonuses that can be gained during game-play. Pac-Man was one of the first games to feature power-ups, in the form of four pellets on the screen. When one of these was gobbled up, the four ghosts giving chase fled and could, for a short time, be eaten by Pac-Man. Power-ups might be included to give a player extra energy, additional lives or a burst of speed.

Game over

At some point, the game has to end. Games creators have to decide how a player can fail. Perhaps they run out of time or get caught by a monster. Many games give characters more than one life, so they can carry on until all their lives are gone.

Fun Features

Some games have options for two players to take part. Others have a 'level save' option, which means that a player does not have to go all the way back to the beginning if they fail on a later level. Other games contain hidden features called 'Easter eggs'. These might be a joke, bonus lives or tips on how to play the game.

TRUE STORY

Penguin Power! An Easter egg inside the Pro Evolution Soccer 6 game allowed players to turn their team of footballers into giant penguins or have their players ride raptor dinosaurs!

Coding Games

Games are computer programs, and each program is made up of lines of computer code. These lines of code tell the computer to perform tasks such as moving an object on the screen or displaying a message.

Learn a language

Lines of code are written in a computer language. Common computer languages for major games include C and C++. Smaller games found on social media or as downloadable **apps** for smartphones are written in languages such as Java or Flash. Popular languages to learn for beginners are Scratch and Kodu.

SCRATCH

Scratch is a free computer language, designed for children and advanced programmers alike. It is made up of colourful blocks, which are the language's commands. These can be clipped together to form a series of instructions called a script.

Scratch features moving objects called sprites. Each sprite can be designed to look like a person, a monster – or whatever object you like. Each sprite can be moved around the screen and instructed to react to other objects by a series of commands.

Getting it right

Whichever computer language coders choose, they have to be patient and very accurate to code the correct movement for an object. You cannot just tell the computer to 'move object A'. You must specify how far the object should move and in what direction.

Scratch Puzzles

Looking at the script, can you solve these puzzles?

1. How would you make the sprite move round in a square shape three times?

2. What two commands would you have to change to make the sprite move round the screen in a triangular shape twice?

This simple Scratch script moves a sprite on a square-shaped path twice.

Script starts when GO! is clicked on the screen.

This block moves the sprite to a point on the screen.

This repeat block causes the sprite to turn and move eight times.

The sprite moves 200 steps in the direction it is facing. Each step is a tiny distance on the screen.

This block pauses movement for one second.

Sprite turns 90 degrees before moving again.

 when GO! clicked

 glide 5 secs to x: 0 y: 100

 repeat 8

 move 200 steps

 wait 1 secs

 turn 90 degrees

Game engines

Major games are very complex and need all their hundreds of different objects to move correctly and realistically. To help out, games developers use a collection (or suite) of programs called a game engine. These programs handle many tasks, including the basic movement, crashes and bounces that objects make in a game. The Unity 3D game engine has been used for hundreds of games, from Angry Birds 2 and Kerbal Space Program to Temple Run and Pokémon GO.

21

Decision Time!

If   Then

As a game is played, its program code is constantly making decisions. If you had to make so many decisions every second, your head would spin! Fortunately, computers are well suited to the task of dealing with lots of information and instructions at the same time.

Algorithms

Algorithms are sets of step-by-step instructions that command a machine to perform a task or solve a problem. Games makers create algorithms to help plan out decisions in games before they write the code.

If ... Then

Many decisions in game algorithms can be written as an 'If ... Then' statement. This means IF something occurs THEN the game will respond in a particular way. In a simple racing game, a car may not be allowed to travel off the track on the screen, so an algorithm in plain English might be:

1. Check position of car.
2. If car on left edge of track, move car right 10 steps.
3. If car on right edge of track, move car left 10 steps.

Crash!

Objects frequently touch or collide in action games. The code has to recognise a collision taking place and decide what happens next. The decisions include figuring out what the character has touched and what that means according to the game's rules.

For example:
IF character touches sweet
THEN remove sweet from screen and add 10 points to score.
or
IF character touches big monster **THEN** stop game, display Game Over and play sad music.

Go with the Flow

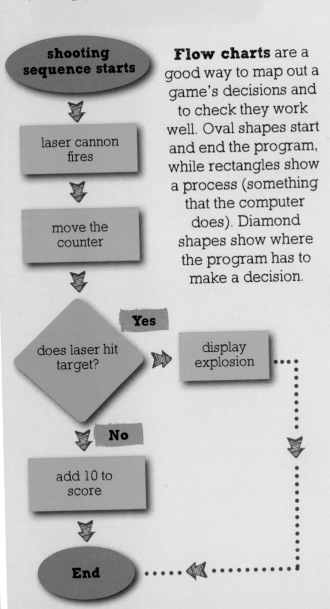

Flow charts are a good way to map out a game's decisions and to check they work well. Oval shapes start and end the program, while rectangles show a process (something that the computer does). Diamond shapes show where the program has to make a decision.

STRETCH YOURSELF

Try Tynkering

Visit https://www.tynker.com/hour-of-code/ to learn about coding in a fun and friendly way. The Tynker programming area contains several simple games. You have to drag command blocks to make them work. The commands are based on Scratch, and help you see how coding and decisions have to be made in games. Try out Scavenger Hunt, Candy Quest and Dragon Dash first.

Controlling Games

All computer games need a way for the player to control the game. For example, players must be able to send instructions to the computer or console to shoot an alien spaceship, pick up a chess piece or make their game character move or jump.

Game controllers

Game controllers are devices used to send instructions to the computer or console. Some games use a computer keyboard or mouse as the controller. Action games tend to be controlled by a joystick or a gamepad.

A joystick is gripped and moved in the direction a player wants their game character to move. Gamepads sometimes have small joysticks or up/down and left/right arrows that do a similar job.

Smartphones and tablets have touchscreens. Games on these machines allow players to use their fingers to make moves, and perform other commands by tapping or swiping the screen.

Custom controllers

Certain games require special controllers. For example, dance games often use a mat that has special switches inside. These send a signal to the computer when a player's foot lands on the button.

Car racing games can be extra fun if played with a physical steering wheel, accelerator and brake pedals, just like a real car.

Complex Controller. One of the most complicated game controllers ever made was built for a robot tank game called Steel Battalion. The controller featured two joysticks, three pedals operated by the player's feet and 40 buttons!

In and Out

All computing, including computer games, rely on three stages. Input is when a user, such as a game player, sends a command or information to the computer or games console. The machine then works or acts on the input in some way. This is called processing. The final stage is when the computer's work is output, such as being displayed on the screen.

Input: Right arrow on gamepad pressed. This sends a signal to the computer

Output: If the character cannot move, the computer might play a bumping sound. If there is space on the right, the character is shown moving across the screen

Processing: Computer recognises input and checks whether character can move right in the game – there might be something in the way

Keeping Score

Part of the fun of many games is trying to beat your own score or the scores set by others. So, most computer games need some sort of scoring system.

Variables

Players gain points in many games by moving over or collecting certain objects. These objects are given a value in points, so a game knows to add them to the player's score.

Points are often stored in a game's code in something called a **variable**. A variable is a small store of information that has a name. This can be accessed and changed by the game's code.

Coins n' Ghosts

In a simple coin-collecting game, players have to avoid ghosts. In English, the code for the game's scoring might look like this:

IF player touches silver coin THEN Score = Score + 5
5 points are added to the score.

IF player touches gold coin THEN Score = Score + 10
10 points are added to the score.

IF player touches ghost THEN Score = Score – 50
50 points are taken away.

 With 10 gold and 10 silver coins, what is the maximum score a player can obtain?

With three ghosts, what is the worst possible score a player can obtain?

High-score history

Early computer games lacked high scores. It wasn't until the arrival of Space Invaders in 1978 that a high score could be saved in computer memory and displayed on screen during the next game. This idea proved a smash hit, as players returned to the game again and again to try to beat the current high score.

Lives left

Many other variables are stored in games. For example, one might keep count of the number of lives a player's character has left. Algorithms in the game decide when a player loses a life, such as when a character falls into water or is caught by a monster.

Sometimes, a variable stores the energy or health of a character. When it reaches zero, it removes one of the player's lives. This might be written as:

IF Energy = 0 THEN Lives = Lives −1

Coding high scores

Storing a high score requires its own variable, which can then be compared to the player's current score, like this (PN is another variable which holds the player's name):

**IF Score > High Score
THEN High Score = Score**

The new score becomes the high score.

Display PN, Display Score

Player's name and high score are shown.

TRUE STORY

Asteroids Champ! All the way back in 1982, 15-year-old Scott Safran set a new high score on the space game Asteroids. His tally of 41,336,440 points wasn't beaten by anyone in the world for 28 years!

Testing and Launching

Even when a major game nears completion, the work is far from over. Coding all the action, movement and features of a game can see lines of code mount up into tens or hundreds of thousands. The game has to be fully tested before launch.

A game needs lots of testing to check it doesn't contain **bugs**. Testing is carried out by the company making the game, but also by the game-playing community. Gamers may **beta test** a game that is almost ready to be launched. They try the game out and report any bugs or areas of the game they feel could be improved.

TRUE STORY

Bugs at Launch! Despite heavy testing, bugs can make it through. In the American football game Madden 15, one of the normally huge 2-metre-tall linebacker players sometimes appears only 30 centimetres tall! In the Nintendo DS game Bubble Bobble Revolution, a bug stopped all players at level 30, not letting them play the game's 70 other levels.

Visitors to Games Week 2016 in Milan, Italy, get to try out the new 3D platform game, Skylanders Imaginators.

Gaining a Rating

In many countries, games have to be sent to an organisation before launch to receive a rating, which advises customers who the game is suitable for based on its content. In the United States, the Entertainment Software Rating Board (ESRB) awards ratings such as E (Everyone can play), E10+, T (Teens and above) and M (Mature audiences, age 17 and over).

Launch time

Major games are launched with a great deal of publicity and sometimes events or stunts. Games are either sold physically as program discs or memory cartridges, or they can be **downloaded** online. Early sales for a well-promoted game can be huge. In 2016, over five million copies of the PlayStation 4 game Final Fantasy XV were sold on the first day. Other games are made available to be downloaded from the Internet.

People playing Pokémon GO. The game was launched in July 2016, and by the end of that month had been downloaded by over 100 million people.

Game over?

The work isn't over after a game is launched. Many coders and other staff might continue to work on the game. They fix any bugs that are found by customers, and may release files called fixes or patches that gamers can download to improve the game.

Sequels and Expansion Packs

Much of the team may start work on a follow-up or sequel to the game, or produce an expansion pack. This is an addition to the original game that adds extra content, such as new characters or more game levels for players to explore. World of Warcraft, for example, has been extended via six expansion packs, including Legion which launched in 2016.

Glossary

3D Short for three-dimensional. A three-dimensional object on screen appears to have depth as well as height and width.

algorithm A set of steps that are followed in order to solve a problem or perform a task.

app A small computer program, such as a game that can be downloaded and used on mobile devices like tablets and smartphones.

assets All the things you can see in a game, including characters, vehicles, tools, weapons and obstacles.

avars Also known as hinge points, these are parts of an animation that can be altered to move part of the animated object.

beta test A test on a game or other computer program to try and discover its faults before it is released.

boss A powerful character in a game that a player must usually defeat at the end of a level.

bug An error in the code of a computer game that produces an unexpected or unwanted result.

console A dedicated machine for playing games, such as an Xbox or PlayStation, which connects to a display monitor or TV screen.

cutscene A scene in a game when gameplay stops (such as when a player completes a level) but movement on the screen continues.

dialogue The words spoken by characters in a computer game or animation.

download To obtain a computer file or program such as a game from another computer often by connecting to it over the Internet.

flow chart A type of diagram that maps out the actions and decisions that occur within a program or part of a program.

game controller The device gamers use to perform actions and commands in a game. Common controllers include a mouse, joystick, gamepad and keyboard.

Internet A network that connects millions of computers all over the world.

massively multi-player online role-playing game (MMORPG) A game in which many individual players control their own characters on a quest in an imaginary world.

memory Part of a computer or other digital device in which information can be stored for use later.

pixels The dots of colour that make up an image on a screen.

porting Adapting a game so that it can be played on lots of different types of device, such as smartphones, tablets and handheld games consoles.

power-up An object in a game that gives the player instant benefits, such as extra lives or more speed.

simulation A game that tries to closely mimic or simulate real-world situations, such as flying an aircraft.

storyboard A visual plan of all the scenes and shots in an animation.

variable A place for storing information in a computer program, which can be changed by other parts of the program.

Further Resources

Books

Kids Get Coding: Games and Animation by Heather Lyons and Alex Westgate (Wayland, 2017)

Go Figure: A Maths Journey Through Computer Games by Hilary Koll and Steve Mills (Wayland, 2016)

Create Computer Games with Scratch by Kevin Wood (Franklin Watts, 2017)

Websites

https://gridclub.com/activities/game-box
Play either a dodge or breakout type game and then build your own with this animated activity which works in Firefox, Safari and Internet Explorer web browsers.

https://scratch.mit.edu/
The homepage of the Scratch programming language, which is great for learning to code simple computer games.

http://www.pbs.org/kcts/videogamerevolution/inside/how/
A website explaining how games are made, with some history on how computer games developed.

http://pixar-animation.weebly.com/three-dimensional-computer-animation.html
Watch behind-the-scenes videos of work at the animated movie company, Pixar.

Answers

page 7
Make History

a) 2009

b) 1994

c) 1981

d) 1972

e) 2006

f) 1983

g) 2005

h) 1989

page 17
Scratch Puzzles

1. Change 'Repeat' to '12'.

2. Change 'Repeat' to '6' and change 'Turn 90 degrees' to 'Turn 120 degrees'.

page 26
Coins n' Ghosts

150 (10 x 10 + 10 x 5)

–150 (3 x -50)

Index

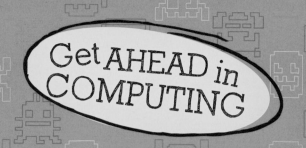
Get AHEAD in COMPUTING

TITLES IN THE SERIES

Computing All Around Us
Input and Output
All About Algorithms
Real-World Algorithms
Sensors
Coding Decisions
In Control
Barcodes and Stock Control
Where Am I?
Money Matters
Working with Robots
3D Printing
The Internet of Things

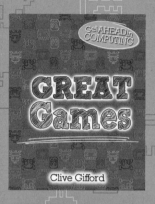

Fun on the Screen
Early Computer Games
Types of Games
Storyboards
Game Assets
Game Characters
The Game World
Game Rules and Features
Coding Games
Decision Time!
Controlling Games
Keeping Score
Testing and Launching

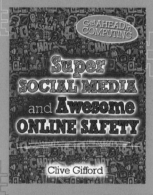

Keeping in Touch
Social Media History
Facebook
Instant Messaging and
  Microblogging
Sharing Snaps
Connecting to Social Media
How Information Spreads
The Business of Social Media
Signing Up and Starting Out
Keeping It Private
Smart, Safe Social Media
Social Media Issues
Cyberbullying

Welcome to the World Wide Web
How the Web Works
The Web Designer's Toolkit
A Selection of Sites
Welcome to HTML
Creating a Page
Adding Images
Jumping Around
Site, Right!
Doing It in Style
Content Management Systems
Design Over time
Added Features

Program Explosion
Operating Systems
Popular Operating Systems
Interface to Face
Data and Circuits
Files in Style
Getting Organised
It's the Business
Text Success
Words and Picture
Sounds and Music
Games, Games, Games
App Attack!

Coding your World
Algorithms in Action
Ones and Zeros
Mind your Language
Languages for Learning
Scratch!
Accurate Algorithms
Get in Step
Decisions, Decisions
Go with the Flow
Going Loopy
A Bug's Life
Coding Careers

A World of Computers
The Incredible
  Shrinking Computer
Here's the Hardware
Let's Look Inside
Data and Circuits
Memory Matters
Imput Devices
More Input Devices
Sounds Amazing
Picture Perfect
Computer Gaming
Mega and Mini Machines

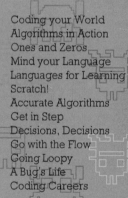

Networks All Around Us
Let's Connect
The Internet
World Wide Web
Web Wonders
A World of Websites
Search Engines
Search and Filter
You've Got Mail
Social Networks
Danger Danger!
Keep It To Yourself